JEDB
KIRKLEES
B.O.F.
1/20

G
35.20 KG   INV
T   155
3.20 KG   84
N
56   KG

SRI LANKA

& 3 &
FELIXS

BOPF
CHOP 339
CHESTS 40/L
1526/1565
GROSS:6.3 KGS
TARE : 5.3 KGS
NETT :51 KGS
LB TEN
51 KGS

Nº 1155...

HAVING TEA

RECIPES & TABLE SETTINGS ◆ TRICIA FOLEY

Photographs by
KEITH SCOTT MORTON

Written by
CATHERINE CALVERT

Design by
RITA MARSHALL

CLARKSON N. POTTER, INC./PUBLISHERS

Grateful acknowledgment is given for the recipes that appear on pages 76 and 77, from *Tea-Time*. Copyright © 1986 by Jane Pettigrew. Reprinted by permission of Dorling Kindersley Publishers Limited.

Photograph appearing on page viii courtesy of the Bettmann Archive.

Photograph appearing on page 73 courtesy of the Newens Maids of Honour Shop, Kew Gardens, England.

Text copyright © 1987 by Tricia Foley
Photographs copyright © 1987 by Keith Scott Morton

Published by Clarkson N. Potter, Inc., 225 Park Avenue South, New York, New York, 10003 and distributed by Crown Publishers, Inc.

CLARKSON N. POTTER, POTTER, and colophon are trademarks of Clarkson N. Potter, Inc.

Manufactured in Japan

Library of Congress Cataloging-in-Publication Data

Foley, Tricia.
  Having tea.
  Includes index.
  1. Tea.   I. Calvert, Catherine.   II.   Title.
GT2905.F64   1987   394.1'2   86-16977
ISBN 0-517-56007-0
10   9   8   7   6

To Gram, for sharing her love of tea

CONTENTS

INTRODUCTION
THE PLEASURES OF TEA   1

STRAWBERRY CREAM TEA   6
SUNDAY AFTERNOON TEA   10
DESSERT PARTY TEA   14
TEA SERVICES   19

TEA ON THE LAWN   22
SUMMER HARVEST PICNIC   26
FALL TEA IN THE COUNTRY   30
THE PERFECT POT OF TEA   35

BRUNCH IN THE CITY   38
TEA BREAK   42
FIRESIDE TEA FOR TWO   46
TEA TASTING   51

THE ENGLISH HOTEL TEA   54
A PROPER CHILDREN'S TEA   58
WINTER HOLIDAY TEA   62
CHRISTMAS EVE TEA   66
THE TEA-ROOM TRADITION   71

THIRTIES-STYLE TEA ROOM   74
THE TEA LARDER   79

MAIL-ORDER TEA SOURCES   83

ACKNOWLEDGMENTS   85

INDEX   86

THE PLEASURES OF TEA

Four o'clock on a winter's afternoon. The dark is drawing in and the spirits, perhaps, ebb with the sun. But, here and there, the kettle's on, water bubbling at a full boil. The kitchen is warm, full of the smell of fresh toast and cinnamon from a just-sliced tea cake, and the tray is laid with, perhaps, some fine tea cups, silver spoons that wink and gleam, fresh napkins. A plate of sunny lemon circles is added and a bowl of sugar and a pitcher of milk. Finally, the fresh brew is ready and poured into the waiting cups. With the first sips, there's contentment, for tea is one of those eternal creature comforts that soothe the body and soul as well as warm the heart.

For a thousand years the leaves of this sturdy evergreen have been steeped and swirled, but there's something about tea that makes it seem just right for us now. Those who are health conscious recognize this as a "natural" drink, simple as the sum of water and leaves and time combined. People shying away from caffeine prefer tea's lighter stimulus, the lift with no corresponding letdown, according to one medical report. The harried crave the restful interlude of tea that comes at the end of a busy day. And not a few wheelers and dealers are finding the "power tea" in big city hotels, with acres of napery and gleaming pots of jam, an effective way to meet a client, negotiate, and make a deal. But the real wealth of the tea table lies in its ability to enrich the everyday, gild the moment with importance, and celebrate the loosening of the day's demands.

Teas are infinitely variable in style. Tea served up in a potbellied brown teapot is cozy, warming as Grandmother's afghan. Tea in a mug is informal, conversational, just right for two friends settling down for a chat and handfuls of cookies. And the full-dress tea, with a glittering silver pot, slivers of tea sandwiches, and little pastel-frosted cakes, makes its partakers sit just a bit straighter and frame their conversations to suit the grand occasion.

Not the least of teatime's pleasures is the ceremony it serves up and the satisfaction of doing something as it has been done for generations. This was the spoon Great-Grandmother used, this was the way we had our cinnamon toast, cut in soldiers or in butterflies, tea served in *this* cup was the magic cure for measles, winter colds, homesickness—all speak of family love as much as the power of orange pekoe.

Taking pains—and time—becomes its own reward. There is a sensual savor to be enjoyed in the aroma of a freshly opened canister of tea, in studding a lemon with cloves and setting it afloat in the cup. Certainly performing such tea ceremonies for guests lets you offer them what often seems in short supply these days —attention and a wish to please.

There's history in the teapot, as well as the water and leaves. The Chinese are to be thanked for the beverage (and for the pot itself). Three thousand years before Christ, their legendary emperor, Shen Nung, is said to have chanced to drink a brew of fresh boiled water and leaves blown into his pot from a nearby

bush, and to have told his people about the miraculous elixir that conquered sleep and cured thirst. By about A.D. 700, the first tea gardens bloomed in Japan, seeded by plants the emperor ordered from China, but five hundred more years were to pass before the taste for tea took root there.

Voyaging Europeans brought tea to Holland, yet another bit of booty from the mysterious East prized at first for its exoticism as well as its use as a stomach restorative. Hostesses of note gathered top society for tea tastings, where fifty cups or more of tea—which cost upward of $100 a pound—accompanied cakes and pipes of tobacco.

But it was the English, of course, who made tea part of their life in ways that continue to the present day. The beverage was late in arriving: The seventeenth-century English were still happily accompanying breakfast with ale and beer, and spending all afternoon in coffeehouses. In 1657, tea was introduced, and the wonder is that it stayed: Some of the confused first purchasers seemed content to brew the leaves and spread them on bread to eat, or to add a bit of butter and salt to the cup. Once again, tea was presented as a magical elixir for health, sure to aid anything from the eyes to the kidneys and, according to its first advertisement, "vanquisheth heavy dreams, easeth the brain, and strengthen Memory." King Charles II returned from exile in Holland with a taste for tea, and his Portuguese queen arrived with tea and teapots as part of her dowry.

The coffeehouses were soon ladling out tea to the wits and layabouts, lords, and lawyers who filled them. Sam Twining himself started a very popular house before he began the tea company his descendants still run. Perhaps tea's best polemicist of the time was Dr. Samuel Johnson, who drank it in such quantities that hostesses offered to serve it to him in a basin. He was, he said, "a hardened and shameless tea-drinker who has for many years diluted his meals with only the infusion of this fascinating plant; whose kettle has scarcely had time to cool; who with tea amuses the evening, with tea solaces the midnight, and with tea welcomes the morning."

Tea came to America with the Dutch and English settlers and was popular in grand houses and backwoods cabins. A Colonial Boston lady would arrive for tea carrying her own precious cup, saucer, and teaspoon in a special little bag. New Yorkers under English rule gathered in tea gardens like those in England, which were sumptuous public pleasure parks where families could buy a pot of tea and while away the time with music and talk, even watching fireworks. Hawkers sold water just for tea all over town. When British taxes on tea abolished any prospect of free trade for the Colonies, women led the first rebellions, banning tea leaves from their tables. Boston Colonists dressed as Indians tossed the cargo of three tea ships into the harbor, the British government closed the port—and American revolutionary sentiments stirred.

By the nineteenth century, the teapot had been de-politicized, and about 1840, tea gained a new ritual in England that's remained popular. Anna, Duchess of Bedford, is said to have originated the afternoon tea as a way to alleviate her "sinking feelings" as she waited for dinner at the fashionably late hour of eight. Sweet and savory tidbits joined the tea table, until the Victorians were tucking into substantial spreads that included groaning cake stands, plates of bright jellies and meringues, and potted meats.

Modern tea takers can borrow from history or make their own choices of what to serve and where and when to serve it. What was once an ordered, formal ritual, full of equipment and detail, circumstance and pomp, can now be the occasion for graceful informality, easy intimacy, wit and warmth. A cup or tray might travel to a desk on a working day, or an elegant tea may be laid in the garden or packed into a wicker hamper for a picnic in a summer field. These days, imagination is the only boundary when it comes to tea.

FOR THREE

Buttermilk Scones, Cream Scones, and Raisin Scones

Grandmother's Strawberry Jam

Whipped Heavy Cream

Fresh Strawberries

Queen Mary Tea

STRAWBERRY CREAM TEA

A tea like this is as English as a Devon hedgerow, where travelers often come upon a farmhouse gate with a sign offering "Cream Teas." There, scones are slathered with clotted cream so heavy it stands on its own, made by heating, then skimming the region's rich milk. A dollop of strawberry jam crowns the peak. This Victorian front porch houses a tea table set with an assortment of heirloom rose-patterned china and a pleasing mix of cutlery—ivory-handled knives and silver teaspoons—gracing embroidered antique linens. The nineteenth-century pot in a sprig pattern holds some mild Queen Mary tea, once blended to that queen's taste.

BUTTERMILK SCONES

The traditional scone can be varied with the addition of raisins. Adding buttermilk gives a slight tang, while cream scones are smooth in taste and texture.

MAKES 12

1¾ cups all-purpose flour
1 teaspoon sugar
1 teaspoon salt
2 teaspoons baking powder
½ teaspoon baking soda
5 tablespoons unsalted butter
Approximately ¾ cup buttermilk

Preheat the oven to 450°F.

Combine the flour, sugar, salt, baking powder, and baking soda in a large bowl and mix thoroughly. Cut in the butter until the mixture resembles coarse crumbs. Add just enough buttermilk to form a soft dough.

Turn out onto a floured board and roll out to ½ inch thick. Cut the dough with a sharp knife into 1½-inch rounds, or use 2-inch cookie cutter and place on an ungreased baking sheet. Bake for 10 to 12 minutes, or until golden brown.

CREAM SCONES

MAKES 8

2 cups all-purpose flour
2 teaspoons sugar
1 teaspoon salt
1 tablespoon baking powder
Approximately 1 cup heavy cream

Preheat the oven to 425°F.

In a large bowl, sift together the dry ingredients. Gradually add enough of the cream to form a soft dough. Knead lightly on a floured board, handling the dough gently to retain the air needed for the scones to rise.

Roll out to a ½- to ¾-inch thickness. Cut into 2-inch rounds with a sharp knife or use a cookie cutter and arrange on an ungreased baking sheet, leaving a ½-inch space around each one. Bake for 10 to 12 minutes, or until golden brown.

RAISIN SCONES

2 cups all-purpose flour
¾ teaspoon baking soda
1½ teaspoons cream of tartar
　Pinch of salt
8 tablespoons (1 stick) chilled unsalted
　butter, cut into small pieces
½ cup raisins
1 egg, beaten
　Approximately ½ cup buttermilk

GLAZE

1 egg yolk
1 tablespoon lukewarm water

Preheat the oven to 425°F.

Combine the flour, baking soda, cream of tartar, and salt in a mixing bowl. Cut in the chilled butter until the mixture resembles fine crumbs. Then add the raisins, beaten egg, and enough buttermilk to make a soft dough. Knead very lightly on a floured board to just combine ingredients, handling gently to retain air needed for scones to rise. Roll out to a ½-inch thickness. Cut the dough into 8 thick wedges with a sharp knife.

Place the scones on 2 greased baking sheets, leaving a ½-inch space around each one. To glaze, combine the egg yolk and water in a bowl and brush onto each scone; be careful not to drip any of the glaze onto the pan or the scones will stick. Bake for 12 to 15 minutes, or until golden brown.

GRANDMOTHER'S STRAWBERRY JAM

This update of an old family recipe has a rich, fruity strawberry flavor.

MAKES ABOUT EIGHT 8-OUNCE JARS.
CAN BE DOUBLED.

4–6 pints ripe strawberries
3 cups sugar
2 teaspoons fresh lemon juice

Wash, dry, and hull the berries. Crush enough berries by hand or by quickly pulsing in a food processor to produce 4 cups.

Pour the puréed berries into a large nonaluminum pot, and stir in the sugar and lemon juice. Bring the mixture to a boil, and simmer over low heat for 9 to 15 minutes, depending on the juiciness of the berries, until the purée begins to thicken. Stir frequently with a stainless-steel spoon.

Remove from the heat and let purée come to room temperature, then cool in the refrigerator for 2 to 3 hours. Simmer again for 9 to 15 minutes to thicken.

Prepare eight 8-ounce glass canning jars by washing, scalding, and draining them; or use the hot-rinse cycle (at least 150°F.) of a dishwasher.

Working quickly, fill the jars to within ½ inch of the top. Wipe the rim with a clean damp cloth and seal with ¼ inch of melted paraffin. Cool the jars overnight. Wipe and seal again if necessary. Store in a cool, dark place.

MENU

Open-Faced Garden Tea Sandwiches
Victorian Poppy Seed Cake
Blackberries and Cream
Red Plums
Darjeeling Tea

RECIPES

SUNDAY AFTERNOON TEA

High summer, sunny Sunday afternoon, and the breeze stirs the organdy curtains near a tea table that's set out to catch the view over a rolling green lawn and welcome guests to a relaxing tea. Fresh garden produce has sparked new changes in the tea sandwich, customarily a simple compilation of filling and soft white bread. These are heartier, more sharply flavored sandwiches—cream cheese and chives on dark pumpernickel bread; cucumbers, sprouts, and lettuce on oatmeal bread; watercress, radishes, and sweet butter on whole grain bread. The breads are home-baked or good quality store-bought loaves. The rich nutty taste of Darjeeling stands up well to the lively flavors of the food.

DARK PUMPERNICKEL BREAD

A slice of this chewy, substantial bread is a good base for open-faced sandwiches.

MAKES ONE 9-INCH LOAF

1 teaspoon active dry yeast
¼ cup warm water
¼ cup sugar
2¾ cups boiling water
4 cups rye flour
1 cup cracked wheat
2 tablespoons salt
2 tablespoons corn oil

Dissolve the yeast in warm water and let stand. Pour the sugar into a heavy 10-inch skillet. Place over medium-high heat for several minutes, tilting the pan back and forth to distribute the sugar until it has melted. Continue to cook until the sugar smokes and turns black (about 2½ minutes). Add the boiling water carefully and slowly and continue stirring with a wooden spoon until the sugar has dissolved. Set aside to cool.

Combine the rye flour, cracked wheat, salt, and corn oil in a large buttered mixing bowl. Pour in the cooled caramel liquid and the dissolved yeast. Beat until the dough is smooth and well blended. Put the dough into a clean, well-oiled bowl, cover with plastic wrap, and let stand for at least four hours at room temperature or in the refrigerator overnight.

Preheat the oven to 200°F.

Press the dough into a flat loaf in a well-greased loaf pan. Cover the pan with aluminum foil and bake for 4 hours. Then raise the oven temperature to 300°F. and bake for an additional 1½ hours, or until the loaf feels firm.

Cool in the pan for 5 minutes; then turn the loaf out on a wire rack to cool completely. Wrap in plastic wrap and refrigerate until chilled. To serve, cut into very thin slices.

OATMEAL BREAD

Here is a rich, sweet bread for garden sandwiches or those on page 81.

MAKES TWO 4 X 9-INCH LOAVES

1½ cups rolled oats (do not use instant)
2 cups boiling water
1 tablespoon active dry yeast
1 teaspoon sugar
½ cup warm water
1 tablespoon salt
¼ cup vegetable oil
¼ cup light molasses
2 cups all-purpose flour
2 to 3 cups whole wheat flour

Put the oats in a large mixing bowl and pour the boiling water over them. Set aside to cool. In another bowl, mix the yeast with the sugar and warm water. When the oats have cooled to lukewarm, add the yeast, salt, oil, molasses, and white flour. Beat well with strong circular strokes. Then add 2 cups of whole wheat flour and begin to knead. Add more whole wheat flour as necessary to make the dough easy to handle. Transfer the dough to a floured board and knead for about 5 minutes.

Return the dough to the bowl, cover with a damp towel, and place in a warm spot until it has doubled in bulk. Punch the dough down, divide it in half, and shape into two loaves. Put them into two 4 x 9-inch well-greased loaf pans, cover loosely with a towel, and place in a warm spot to rise again for 30 to 40 minutes, until the dough approaches the top of the pans. Preheat the oven to 350°F.

Bake the loaves for 45 minutes to 1 hour, or until they are browned and hollow when tapped on the bottom.

VICTORIAN POPPY SEED CAKE

This solid, satisfying cake was typical of a hearty Victorian tea. Fresh lavender may be used for decoration.

MAKES ONE BUNDT CAKE
OR 10-INCH TUBE CAKE

½ cup dark poppy seeds
½ cup milk
¾ pound (3 sticks) unsalted butter,
    softened
1½ cups granulated sugar
2 tablespoons grated lime rind
1 tablespoon grated orange rind
8 eggs, separated, at room temperature
2 cups sifted cake flour
¾ teaspoon salt

SYRUP (OPTIONAL)
¼ cup fresh lime juice
¼ cup fresh orange juice
⅓ cup superfine sugar

Soak the poppy seeds in the milk for 4 hours or more. Rinse the seeds under cold running water, and then drain well.

Preheat the oven to 350°F. Grease and flour a Bundt pan or a 10-inch tube pan.

Cream the butter and gradually beat in 1¼ cups granulated sugar. Beat in the grated lime and orange rinds and poppy seeds. Add the egg yolks, one at a time, beating well after each addition. Continue beating for about 5 minutes, or until the mixture is very light and creamy.

In a large mixing bowl, beat the egg whites until soft peaks form. Add the remaining ¼ cup granulated sugar and beat until the peaks are stiff but not dry.

Sift the flour and salt over the egg yolk mixture a third at a time, folding in after each addition. Gently fold in a quarter of the egg whites; then fold in the rest.

Pour the batter carefully into the prepared pan. Bake 1 hour, or until a toothpick comes out clean when tested in the center. If you like a tangy cake, make a syrup by combining the lime juice and orange juice in a glass measuring cup; stir in the superfine sugar until it has completely dissolved.

Cool the cake in the pan on a wire rack for 10 minutes, then unmold, or if using a syrup, immediately upon removing the cake from the oven, prick the top with a long-tined fork or thin skewer. Pour the lime and orange juice–sugar syrup all over the top to cover it completely. Cool in the pan to allow the syrup to soak in and add a tangy flavor.

DESSERT PARTY TEA

M E N U

FOR FOUR

Raspberry Sorbet with Spearmint

Lemon Curd Tartlets

Raspberry Shortcake with Whipped Cream

Sugar Cookies
(SEE PAGE 45)

Prince of Wales Tea

DESSERT PARTY TEA

Gathering friends around on a sun-dappled day for a feast of sweet treats is a grand indulgence, but those who eat heartily can ease their conscience by remembering that the tea itself, without milk or sugar, has no calories. The rest of the table, however, is toppling with riches, served up on a pattern of Staffordshire that's been popular since the mid-nineteenth century, with linens and flower arrangements lavish in country charm. The tea that might stand up to this assortment of sweets is a hearty Prince of Wales. The ripe raspberries of the season inspire the recipes.

RASPBERRY SORBET WITH SPEARMINT

For a tangier sorbet, use only 1½ cups sugar.

SERVES 12

6 cups fresh raspberries, cleaned, hulled,
   and dried
2 cups sugar
2¼ cups fresh strained orange juice
1 teaspoon finely chopped, fresh
   spearmint leaves, plus several whole
   leaves
⅓ cup Triple Sec liqueur

Combine the raspberries, sugar, orange juice, and chopped spearmint leaves in a large bowl. Allow to marinate for 1 hour.

Put the mixture into a blender or food processor and purée. Stir in the Triple Sec. Then pour the mixture into two ice-cube trays with the ice-cube sections removed (or pans of similar size). Freeze until not quite firm; then scoop the mixture back into the blender or food processor and beat until just slushy. Return the mixture to the trays until almost firm and beat again in the blender or food processor. Freeze and

beat again, this time allowing the sorbet to freeze almost solid. (Note: If your sorbet freezes completely, let it soften in the refrigerator for about 30 minutes before serving.) Garnish each serving with whole spearmint leaves.

LEMON CURD TARTLETS

An almond-flavored cookie crust goes well with the sharp flavor of lemon.

MAKES 16

TARTLET CRUST

½ cup confectioners' sugar
½ pound (2 sticks) unsalted butter
1 teaspoon vanilla extract
2 cups all-purpose flour
   Pinch of salt
½ cup blanched almonds, finely chopped

LEMON CURD (MAKES 2 CUPS)

3 eggs
5 tablespoons butter, melted
1 cup granulated sugar
   Juice and finely grated rind of
   2 lemons

To make the crust, in a large bowl, cream the sugar and butter. Add the vanilla and beat well. Mix in the flour, salt, and almonds to form an even-textured dough. Divide the dough in half and wrap each in aluminum foil; refrigerate for at least 1 hour.

Preheat the oven to 325°F. To bake the tartlets, use either miniature muffin pans or tartlet molds; grease them well. Roll out the dough, half at a time, to about a ⅛-inch thickness. For a 1½-inch pan, cut 16 pieces of dough, using a sharp knife or a 2-inch cookie cutter. Press the dough firmly into the pans. Bake for 25 minutes. Cool completely before filling.

To make the lemon curd, beat the eggs into the melted butter; then stir in the sugar. Beat until thoroughly combined. Add the lemon juice and rind gradually. Cook in the top of a double boiler over simmering water until thickened, stirring constantly. Let cool before pouring into the baked tartlets. Extra curd can be stored in the refrigerator for a week and used as a spread on bread or cookies.

RASPBERRY SHORTCAKE

A proper shortcake is a buttery, bis-cuitlike cake, to be split and filled at the last moment.

SERVES 8

2 cups sifted all-purpose flour
¼ cup granulated sugar
1 tablespoon baking powder
    Pinch of salt

8 tablespoons (1 stick) unsalted butter,
    cut into bits
1 egg plus enough milk to measure
    ¾ cup

RASPBERRY FILLING

2 pints heavy cream, whipped
1 tablespoon confectioners' sugar
1 teaspoon vanilla extract
1 pint raspberries, cleaned, hulled, and
    dried

Preheat the oven to 400°F. Grease an 8 x 1½-inch round layer pan.

In a bowl, combine flour, sugar, baking powder, and salt. Cut the butter into the flour mixture until it resembles coarse meal. Mix the egg and milk. Then make a well in the center of the flour-butter mixture and pour in the egg and milk. Stir but do not overmix; there should be a few lumps.

Put the dough into the prepared pan very gently, making sure the dough is evenly distributed. Bake for at least 25 minutes. Test the center with a toothpick to see if it comes out clean. To remove, gently loosen the edges of the shortcake with a knife. Turn out onto a wire rack to cool.

Cut the cake in half to make two layers. Cover the bottom half with whipped cream flavored with the confectioners' sugar and vanilla extract. On top of the whipped cream, add a generous layer of raspberries. Place the top half of the shortcake over the raspberries and cream. Spread the top of the cake with the remaining whipped cream and sprinkle with the remaining raspberries.

TEA SERVICES

The trappings of the tea table have always reflected wealth and social standing, as well as the owner's personal style and the history of the beverage itself. It's evolution, not accident, that gives us teapots with a low-slung bulge, cups with handles, and saucers with sloping sides. Today we may pour from Granny's Rococo revival silver, with its matching tray, creamer, and sugar bowl, and display a rare New Hall porcelain pot with its delicate flowers, or a wildly colored Art Deco

ceramic piece. Teaware both serves and signals taste and needs.

The first tea containers came from China, which was years ahead of Europe in mastering the potters' arts. The Chinese brewed their tea in the kettle or in a cup, until about 1500, during the Ming Dynasty, when potters of Yi-Xing, near Shanghai, began to make pots of unglazed brown or red stoneware for tea. The earliest teapots imitated ceremonial wine vessels in their shape, but experimentation led to the handle being placed at the top, and the pot itself taking on increasingly fanciful forms, like fruit and flowers. By the end of the century, the Chinese were making their teaware of porcelain, that fine, glazed, hard "china." Packed into the holds of trade ships, Chinese porcelain carried Chinese style and motifs to Europe.

It was a hundred years before Europeans found the clue to making simple unglazed earthenware, and many more years passed before porcelain was produced. Europeans often decorated their china with the Oriental motifs they'd always prized—willoware being one of the surviving examples. The Germans at Meissen, the French at Sèvres produced exquisite tea services, but it is in England, where the habit of tea drinking became more firmly established, that master porcelain makers like Wedgwood and Spode evolved extensive designs to serve the taste for tea at all class and price levels.

By the middle of the eighteenth century, tea drinking had become high fashion. Hostesses began to de-

mand tea sets that matched and required a whole equipage to serve their guests properly. Slop bowls in which to pour out the dregs of tea, sugar bowls, creamers, sugar tongs, and caddies and boxes to store the precious substance under lock and key were made to individual requirements. Cups were small, like those the Chinese used, though pouring one's tea into a cup's high-rimmed saucer to sip was no disgrace—having "a dish of tea" remained popular well into the next century. As cake stands and bread-and-butter plates became part of the tea table's wares, one writer commented in 1744 that maintaining a fashionable tea table was more expensive than providing for two children and a nurse.

Tea lovers could choose from increasingly costly materials and fanciful designs. Changing tastes and changing times were reflected here as elsewhere: The simple lines of Regency silver pots, for instance, contrast with the elaborate designs of Victorian examples. Pots were shaped like cauliflowers, or emblazoned with mottoes, or were crafted of silver: Stuart's sensitive portrait of silversmith Paul Revere pictures him with a teapot. Fine cabinetmakers, like Chippendale, produced exquisite tea caddies (their name derived from the Malay word *catty,* a measure of 1⅔ pounds), with perhaps, a mixing bowl within, so a hostess could mix different tea varieties and serve her guests to their tastes. All these triumphs of craftsmanship are now among the most desired of antiques, recalling the luxury and tradition of teas past.

MENU

FOR TWO

Sugar-Glazed Lemon Cake

Walnut Tea Loaf

Peach-Orange Jam

Fresh Apricots

Sweet Butter

Black Currant Tea

TEA ON THE LAWN

Sunlight sweeps the tea table for an afternoon tea on the lawn—a break from the quiet pleasures of reading, gardening, or walking down a country lane. The shell motif on much of the silver and cutlery is a two-centuries-old design, reflecting the eighteenth-century taste for the simple, the classical in teaware. Two good friends might watch the shadows lengthen through the afternoon as they nibble at the cake, spread a walnut loaf with fresh preserves, and share a pot of black currant tea.

SUGAR-GLAZED LEMON CAKE

This classic English recipe produces a cake that is light and lemony, with a bit of an almond crunch.

MAKES ONE 10-INCH LOAF OR BUNDT CAKE

½ pound (2 sticks) unsalted butter, softened
1 cup granulated sugar
Grated rind of 2 lemons
1 tablespoon lemon juice
1 cup sour cream
2 teaspoons vanilla extract
6 egg whites
Pinch of salt
2 cups all-purpose flour
1 teaspoon baking powder
1 cup blanched almonds, finely chopped

SYRUP

¼ cup lemon juice
¼ cup water
½ cup packed dark brown sugar

Preheat the oven to 350°F. Grease and flour a Bundt pan or a 10-inch tube pan.

In a bowl, cream the butter with ½ cup sugar. Beat in the lemon rind, lemon juice, sour cream, and vanilla.

In another bowl, beat the egg whites with the salt until stiff. Gradually beat in the remaining ½ cup sugar.

In a third bowl, mix together the flour and baking powder. Stir in the dry ingredients into the butter mixture, along with a third of the egg whites. Gently add the rest of the egg whites and stir until thoroughly folded in. Mix in the almonds.

Carefully pour the batter into the prepared pan. Bake for 1 hour and 10 minutes, or until a toothpick comes out clean when tested in the center. To make a syrup, combine the lemon juice, water, and brown sugar in a pan, and cook, stirring over very low heat, until the sugar is completely dissolved.

Immediately upon removing the cake from the oven, prick the top with a long-tined fork or thin skewer and pour the lemon juice–brown sugar syrup all over the top to cover it completely. Cool in the pan to let the tangy syrup soak in.

WALNUT TEA LOAF

Tea loaves are usually easy to slice and not too sweet.

MAKES 2 LOAVES

1⅓ cups honey
12 tablespoons (1½ sticks) butter or margarine, melted and cooled
2 eggs
½ cup milk
2 tablespoons lemon or lime juice
3½ cups all-purpose flour
¾ teaspoon baking soda
¼ teaspoon salt
1 teaspoon ground cloves
1 cup walnuts, coarsely chopped
½ cup diced candied orange peel or mixed peel (available in specialty food shops)

Preheat the oven to 325°F. Grease and flour two 8½ x 4½-inch loaf pans.

In a large bowl combine the honey, butter, eggs, milk, and lemon or lime juice with a wooden spoon until well blended.

In a separate bowl, stir together the flour, baking soda, salt, and cloves. Add the flour mixture to the honey mixture and beat until light and creamy. Mix in the walnuts and orange peel. Pour into the prepared loaf pans, spreading the batter evenly. Tap the pan bottoms sharply against a hard surface a few times to settle the batter.

Bake for 1 hour, or until a toothpick comes out clean when inserted in the center. Cool the loaves in the pans on wire racks for about 10 mintues; then turn them out of the pans and cool completely on the racks.

PEACH-ORANGE JAM

These preserves are a subtle blend of sweet peaches and tangy oranges.

MAKES ABOUT TEN 8-OUNCE JARS.
CAN BE DOUBLED.

Approximately 5 pounds fresh peaches
3 oranges
4½ cups sugar
Juice of ½ large lemon

Wash and dry the peaches, but do not peel them. Pit the peaches and coarsely chop them into large chunks either by hand or with a food processor. You should have 8 cups.

Finely grate the zest from one of the oranges. Peel all of the oranges and remove as much of the white pith as you can. Quarter the oranges and coarsely chop by hand or in a food processor.

In a large nonaluminum pot, combine the peaches, orange zest, oranges, sugar, and lemon juice. Cook over low heat for 2½ hours, stirring often with a stainless-steel spoon to prevent sticking.

Prepare ten 8-ounce glass canning jars (see page 9) and, working quickly, fill them to within ½ inch of the top. Wipe the edges with a clean damp cloth. Seal with ¼ inch of melted paraffin. Cool the jars overnight. Wipe and seal again if necessary.

Honey-Glazed Chicken with Rosemary

Red Potato Salad

Vine-Ripened Tomatoes with Fresh Basil

Crusty White Peasant Bread

Old-Fashioned Peach Pie

Fresh Peaches

Minted Iced Orange Pekoe Tea

RECIPES

SUMMER HARVEST PICNIC

When the farmstands are brimming with rosy tomatoes, lush bunches of herbs, and fragrant peaches, it's the perfect time to celebrate the last days of summer. This is a hearty hamperful of foods that could make up a "high tea," an early supper, to be carried off to a grassy slope as the evening turns fresh and cool. A container of iced orange pekoe steeped with mint adds its own bracing, invigorating touch.

HONEY-GLAZED CHICKEN
WITH ROSEMARY

Sweet, yet sharp, this glaze is full of rosemary's savor.

SERVES 4

- 2 tablespoons roughly chopped, fresh rosemary leaves
- 1/4 cup wild flower honey
- 2 teaspoons good grainy French mustard
- 2 small or 1 large clove garlic, finely chopped
- 1/4 cup good olive oil
- 2 tablespoons lime or lemon juice
  A generous amount of freshly ground black pepper
  Salt to taste
- 1 4-pound chicken, cut into small serving pieces

Combine all the ingredients and coat the chicken pieces thoroughly. Broil or grill slowly and turn often while the pieces are cooking, making sure not to overcook to retain moistness. Serve cold.

RED POTATO SALAD

Leaving the skin on the tiny new potatoes gives this salad color and texture.

SERVES 4

- 8 small Red Bliss potatoes (approximately 1 1/2 pounds)
- 3 heaping tablespoons finely chopped scallions
- 2 teaspoons fresh tarragon leaves, finely chopped, or 2/3 teaspoon dry tarragon
- 2 heaping tablespoons mayonnaise (homemade or store-bought)
- 1/4 cup sour cream
- 2 teaspoons prepared white horseradish
  Juice of 1 small lemon or lime
  Salt and pepper to taste

Scrub the potatoes well; then steam them in their jackets until they are just tender. (Do not overcook them.)

Cut the potatoes into bite-size pieces. Combine the remaining ingredients and mix them into the potatoes while they are still warm. Cover and refrigerate for at least 1 hour before serving to allow the flavors to blend. Store in the refrigerator if preparing in advance.

VINE-RIPENED
TOMATOES
WITH FRESH BASIL

SERVES 4

*3 large fresh, vine-ripened tomatoes,
    thickly sliced (enough for about 3
    layers in a wide dish)*
*2 tablespoons finely chopped scallions, or
    1 tablespoon chopped chives*
*2 heaping tablespoons finely chopped
    fresh basil leaves*
Good peanut or olive oil
*Good red or white unflavored wine
    vinegar*
Coarse salt

Layer the sliced tomatoes in a wide
serving dish. Sprinkle with the scallions
or chives and basil, distributing them
well. Add a generous dribble of oil and
1 tablespoon (or a little more to taste) of
wine vinegar. Sprinkle with salt. Can be
served immediately or kept for 1 to 2
hours at room temperature to let flavors
steep.

OLD-FASHIONED
PEACH PIE

Fresh grated nutmeg adds both fragrance and flavor.

MAKES ONE 9-INCH PIE

PIE CRUST

*12 tablespoons (1 1/2 sticks) chilled unsalted
    butter, cut into small pieces*
2 cups all-purpose flour
1/4 teaspoon salt (optional)
2 tablespoons sugar
2 egg yolks
2 to 4 tablespoons ice water

FILLING

5–6 cups peeled, thinly sliced ripe peaches
2 tablespoons Triple Sec liqueur
*1/4–1/2 cup sugar (depending on the
    sweetness of the peaches)*
1 teaspoon grated lemon zest

To make the crust, combine the
butter with the flour, salt, and sugar
using two knives or a pastry blender,
until the texture resembles coarse meal.
Beat the egg yolks and ice water
together and add to the butter-flour
mixture, stirring quickly with a fork; add
more water as needed for elasticity.

Form the dough into two balls and
cover each with wax paper. Chill for 1
hour. Preheat the oven to 375°F.

Roll out one ball of dough and line a
9-inch pie pan with it.

To make the filling, sprinkle the
Triple Sec over the peaches and toss to
moisten. Sprinkle the sugar on top of
the tossed peaches and toss again to coat
with sugar. Pour the filling into the pie
shell and sprinkle with the grated lemon
rind.

Roll out the remaining dough and
place over the peach filling. Trim the
edges and crimp decoratively. Cut 4 or 5
small slits in the top crust to make steam
vents.

Reduce the heat to 350°F. Place the
pie on a baking sheet with sides and
bake in the center of the oven for 30 to
40 minutes, until brown.

MINTED ICED
ORANGE PEKOE TEA

Add fresh spearmint leaves to the
loose orange pekoe tea before pouring
the boiling water into the teapot. Let
it steep for at least 1/2 hour. Strain, chill,
and serve with a sprig of fresh
spearmint leaves.

M E N U

Individual Flans

Cheshire and Stilton Cheeses

Crusty White Peasant Bread

Yellow Cherry Tomatoes

Greengage Plums

Individual Apple Tarts

Cider and Lapsang Souchong Tea

FALL TEA IN THE COUNTRY

On an autumn afternoon, when the air has the snap and tang of the season's first apples, a country drive is called for. Sharpened appetites will delight in this lavish supply of food spread on a tartan rug. The tea—strong, smoky Lapsang Souchong. Brew it at home and keep it hot in a thermos. Country English cheeses and the first of the fall fruits complement a variety of flans, and all tuck into traditional wicker hampers for transport.

INDIVIDUAL FLANS

This basic flan recipe is infinitely variable and can be made with whatever vegetables are freshest at the market.

MAKES FOUR 4-INCH FLANS
FLAN SHELLS

9 tablespoons (1⅛ sticks) chilled unsalted butter, cut into small pieces
1½ cups all-purpose flour
1 egg yolk
3 tablespoons ice water
Pinch of salt (optional)

BASIC FLAN CUSTARD

1½ cups heavy cream
3 large eggs
Salt and freshly ground black pepper to taste
Freshly ground nutmeg

FLAN FILLINGS

ZUCCHINI FLAN

1 medium yellow onion, thickly sliced and sautéed in butter until translucent
2 small zucchinis, coarsely chopped and sautéed quickly in butter until crisp-tender
1 teaspoon chopped fresh tarragon leaves, or ½ teaspoon dried tarragon
Pinch of cayenne pepper
2 cups grated Gruyère cheese

HAM AND CHEESE

½ pound hickory smoked ham, finely chopped
½ cup onion, sliced and sautéed in butter until translucent
1 cup grated Cheddar cheese

CHEESE, LEEK, AND SPINACH

½ cup chopped leeks (white part only), well rinsed and sautéed in butter until translucent
1 pound fresh spinach, or one 10-ounce package frozen spinach (defrosted and well drained)
1 tablespoon chopped fresh dill leaves
4 ounces feta cheese
¾ cup grated Swiss cheese

To make the pastry shells, mix the flour and salt, then cut in the butter, using two knives; work quickly until the mixture resembles coarse meal.

In another bowl, combine the egg yolk and ice water. Add this to the flour-butter mixture and stir briefly to get a moist, even dough. Gather into a ball, wrap in aluminum foil, and chill for 1 hour. Roll out dough to ¼-inch thickness, then lightly press it into individual pie pans, cover, and chill for at least 1 hour.

Preheat the oven to 375°F.

When chilled, prick the bottoms of the shells with a fork, line the insides with lightweight aluminum foil, and fill them with dried beans or aluminum baking pellets. Bake for 10 minutes, or until the edges of the crusts are slightly browned.

Remove from the oven and remove the foil and beans or pellets. Cool on wire racks.

To make the custard, mix together all the ingredients in a bowl. Set aside until ready to add to the shell with the filling.

To make the filling, combine all the ingredients for the one of your choice.

Preheat the oven to 350°F.

To assemble the flans, place one quarter of the filling in each shell, distributing it evenly over the crusts. Pour the custard on top, leaving a ¼-inch space below the rim of the crusts to prevent overflow. Gently shift the pans so that the custard can seep through.

Bake for 30 to 40 minutes, or until the custard is set. Let stand for 5 minutes before serving.

Individual Apple Tarts

The crunch of well-toasted puff pastry contrasts nicely with lightly sugared baked apple slices.

MAKES 4

Puff pastry, homemade or frozen packaged
2 large tart apples (Granny Smiths, for example)
2 tablespoons lemon or lime juice
¼ teaspoon ground cloves or cinnamon
2 tablespoons light brown sugar
4 tablespoons apricot preserves
½ cup walnuts, finely chopped (optional)
2 tablespoons (¼ stick) unsalted butter, melted

Roll out the puff pastry to an 11-inch square. (If using frozen pastry, thaw for 20 minutes or more before rolling out.) Divide into four 5½-inch circles, cutting around the edges with a sharp knife. Put the pastry on a large ungreased baking sheet and refrigerate for at least 20 minutes.

Preheat the oven to 425°F.

Peel and core the apples and cut them into ⅛-inch slices. Toss with lemon or lime juice, cloves or cinnamon, and brown sugar.

Cover each circle of pastry with 1 tablespoon of the apricot preserves. Then place a row of apple slices on top of each pastry circle (see photograph), leaving a ¾-inch border on all sides. Place a slice at the top and bottom of each pastry circle and invert the last slice in the row to form a complete circle of apple slices on top of the pastry. Turn up the pastry edges to form a shell. Brush with the melted butter.

To prevent scorching, place the baking sheet of pastries on a second baking sheet. Bake for 25 to 35 minutes, or until the crusts are crisp and golden. Cool on wire racks before serving.

THE PERFECT POT OF TEA

Brewing up a pot of tea can be one of life's pleasures: There's the comforting circle of ritual and tradition, there's the opportunity to hold and handle a pretty pot, a precious cup, there's the savor of steeping leaves and a curl of steam warming the room on a cold day. Taking the time to do it all properly yields rewards beyond those achieved by the quick dunk of a tea bag in a mug. And it yields a better brew.

Like any ceremony that's been with us for a few centuries, not all of its practitioners agree on technique. Even the British turned the question over to their Standards Institute—and got directions that satisfied nobody. But this, in brief, is a compilation of folk wisdoms and authoritative advice for the perfect pot of tea.

✦ There's no need to get fanatical about the water (though in the earliest days of New York City, special pumps just for tea water were set up for the populace). But be sure to draw the water from the cold tap, so it's fresh and full of oxygen.

✦ Select a good-quality tea. Remember that different types of tea leaves require slightly different brewing times, and the tiny little tea leaves in bags require scarcely any time in the water.

✦ If you're packing a tea ball or infuser, don't fill it to the brim; tea leaves need space to expand as they steep.

✦ Choose any proper pot, from a homely brown pottery potbellied friend to Great-Grandmother's silver. But avoid aluminum or hard worn enamel on metal, as either will taint the tea's flavor.

✦ Swirl a bit of hot water in the pot and then pour out the water. A warm pot will help keep the water at the boiling point, crucial for proper brewing.

✦ If you're using the tea loose, the received wisdom is to add one teaspoonful of tea for each person to be served, and one for the pot. But experience, as well as your choice of tea, may advise dipping out only half that amount. Few people, however, like their tea very weak, and it's easy to dilute a strong cup with fresh hot water.

✦ Bring the teapot to the kettle on the stove as the water reaches boiling—a true boil. The less distance the kettle must travel, the more likely the water is to stay boiling. Do not, however, let it continue bubbling on the fire; those bubbles are carrying away all the oxygen, and overboiled water leads to tea with a markedly muddy taste.

✦ Let the tea steep, or "mash" as they say in the north of England. Normally, steeping time is about 5 minutes for taste, flavor, and color to bloom, but small-leaved teas, like a green tea, take a much shorter time, while a hearty Lapsang Souchong might need 7 or 8 minutes.

✦ Give the mixture a stir and then serve, after removing the infuser, or, if you've simply used the tea loose in the pot, place a strainer between the spout and the cups.

BRUNCH IN THE CITY

M E N U

Toasted Cornmeal Muffins with Apple Butter
Slow-Scrambled Eggs with Cream and Chives
Pan-Fried Tomatoes with Fresh Tarragon
Honeydew Melon Wedges with Lemon
Bloody Marys and English Breakfast Tea

BRUNCH IN THE CITY

Tea in this light-filled loft is served in a fine assortment of contemporary hand-crafted teapots and cups, full of wit and whimsy in their use of twisted and molded clay. The brunch menu centers on sumptuous slow-scrambled eggs, which contrast with the crispy, toasted corn muffins and make a fine start to a lazy Sunday. An accompanying cup of English Breakfast tea, with its smooth, strong flavor, is tempered with the traditional serving of milk and sugar.

CORNMEAL MUFFINS

The fragrant muffins are even better split, buttered, and toasted.

MAKES 12

1 cup all-purpose flour
4 teaspoons baking powder
¾ cup stoneground cornmeal
¼ cup rolled oats, quick-cooking or old-fashioned
Salt to taste
2 large eggs
⅓ cup maple syrup
¾ cup buttermilk
Dash of cayenne pepper
¼ cup of marmalade (optional)

Preheat the oven to 400°F.

In a large bowl, mix the flour, baking powder, cornmeal, rolled oats, and salt with a fork until blended.

In another bowl, beat the eggs well with a fork or whisk. Add the maple syrup, buttermilk, and cayenne pepper (to enhance the muffins' flavor but not make them hot), and beat very well. Add the dry ingredients to this mixture, folding them in gently to keep in air so that the muffins will rise; the batter should be rough and lumpy. Spoon the batter into greased muffin pans, until they are three-quarters full.

If you like, you can add marmalade to the muffins before baking by gently making a well in the top of each one and dropping in ¾ teaspoon of marmalade. Bake for 12 to 15 minutes, or until the muffins feel firm. Remove immediately from the pans and cool on a wire rack.

SLOW-SCRAMBLED EGGS WITH CREAM AND CHIVES

The tang of fresh chives is worth a search of the market, but parsley or dill makes an admirable alternative.

SERVES 3

4 tablespoons (½ stick) salted butter
6 eggs
¼ cup heavy cream
Dash of salt to taste
Chives

Melt the butter in the top of a double boiler over low heat. Remove from the heat and let the butter cool for five minutes. Return the double boiler to the heat, break the eggs into the pot, and add the cream. Cook slowly over barely simmering water, slowly folding the egg mixture into large curds or peaks. Remove from the heat, season with salt, and garnish with freshly cut chives. Serve immediately.

APPLE BUTTER

This is best made with fresh pressed cider—the kind sold at farmer's markets.

MAKES THREE TO FIVE 8-OUNCE JARS

2 pounds apples (preferably strongly flavored ones such as Jonathan, Winesap, or Granny Smith)
1 cup good apple cider
Approximately 2½ cups dark brown sugar (see below for amount)
1 teaspoon ground cinnamon
½ teaspoon ground allspice
¼ teaspoon ground ginger
½ teaspoon ground cloves
1 teaspoon fresh lemon juice
1 tablespoon grated lemon zest
2 teaspoons port wine

Core the apples and quarter them, but do not peel. Mix with apple cider and cook until soft. Put pulp through a fine strainer. For every cup of pulp, add ½ cup dark brown sugar. Then add the remaining ingredients. Cook, stirring the fruit mixture at a low simmer until the sugar is dissolved; do not boil. Continue stirring until the apple butter starts to set. To test for doneness, place a small amount on a plate; when no rim of liquid separates around the edge of the butter, it is ready.

Remove the apple butter from heat, pour into five 8-ounce hot sterilized glass canning jars, and fill and seal (see instructions page 9).

PAN-FRIED TOMATOES WITH FRESH TARRAGON

Choose hard, sliceable red tomatoes or, for a delicious variation, try green ones.

SERVES 4

2 large ripe red tomatoes
1 tablespoon salted butter
1 tablespoon olive oil
1 tablespoon chopped fresh tarragon
Freshly ground black pepper to taste
Dash of cayenne pepper
Sprigs of fresh tarragon, for garnish

Slice the tomatoes ¼ to ½ inch thick. In a large frying pan over medium heat, heat the butter and olive oil. Add the tomatoes and sprinkle with tarragon, black pepper, and cayenne pepper. When the tomatoes have browned on one side (about 2 to 3 minutes), flip them; make sure they are cooked through. Garnish with fresh tarragon and serve.

BLOODY MARYS

SERVES 3

½ cup vodka
9 ounces tomato juice
9 ounces V-8 juice
1½ teaspoons prepared horseradish
3 tablespoons Worcestershire sauce
Tabasco, celery salt, and pepper to taste
Ice

Combine vodka, juices, and sauces in a large pitcher. Stir well and season to taste. Serve over ice in large goblets.

MENU

Spicy Ginger Bundt Cake

Aunt Sally's Bundt Cake

Sugar Cookies

Basket of Cherries

Thermos of Hot Earl Grey Tea

TEA BREAK

"Tea . . . will always be the favored beverage of the intellectual," wrote Thomas de Quincy, and a break for tea in a hideaway like this is a solace as well as a stimulant. Tea, though a beverage that suits a social occasion, is a satisfying companion for a solitary moment, especially when partnered with a few tea treats. Take the time to place some sugar cookies on an elegant plate, slice a bit of ginger or streusel-laced Bundt cake, and put out a proper napkin. Tea for one, with the faintly citrus flavor of Earl Grey, is the reverie's reward. Brewing the tea, then keeping it hot in a thermos, means that work needn't be interrupted by trips to the kitchen.

SPICY GINGER BUNDT CAKE

Ginger's the topnote, but cinnamon, allspice, nutmeg, and cloves add their flavors.

MAKES ONE 10-INCH BUNDT CAKE

½ pound (2 sticks) salted butter, softened
2 scant cups packed dark brown sugar
3 eggs
⅓ cup honey
⅓ cup light corn syrup
1 cup sour cream
¼ cup Triple Sec or other orange or
*   tangerine liqueur*
½ cup fresh lemon juice
1⅔ cups all-purpose flour
1 cup whole wheat flour
4 teaspoons baking powder
1 teaspoon ground cinnamon
1 teaspoon ground allspice
2½ teaspoons chopped crystallized ginger
1 teaspoon ground nutmeg
1 teaspoon ground cloves
½ cup dark raisins
1 cup walnuts, roughly chopped, or 1 cup
*   blanched slivered almonds*

Preheat the oven to 350°F. Grease and flour a 10-inch Bundt pan.

In a bowl, cream the butter with the brown sugar. Beat in the eggs, honey, corn syrup, sour cream, liqueur, and lemon juice.

In another bowl, mix together the white and whole wheat flours, baking powder, and spices. Add to the butter mixture. Stir in the raisins and nuts.

Pour into the prepared pan. Bake for 1½ hours, or until a toothpick comes out clean when inserted in the center. Remove from pan and cool on wire rack. The cake keeps well; it will remain very moist and flavorful if wrapped in wax paper, placed in a cake tin, and stored in a cool, dry cupboard.

Aunt Sally's Bundt Cake

This rich, simple Bundt cake, a family favorite, is an alternate indulgence.

MAKES ONE 10-INCH BUNDT CAKE

12 tablespoons (1½ sticks) unsalted butter, softened
1½ cups sugar
5 eggs
1 cup sour cream
1 teaspoon vanilla
2 teaspoons baking powder
1 teaspoon baking soda
½ teaspoon salt (optional)
3 cups flour, sifted 3 times

STREUSEL

½ cup sugar
1 ounce (1 square) unsweetened chocolate or 1 ounce cocoa
1 teaspoon ground cinnamon
¾ cup finely chopped nuts

Preheat oven to 350°F. Butter and flour a 10-inch Bundt pan.

In a bowl, cream the butter and sugar until fluffy, about five minutes. Add the eggs, one at a time, beating well after each addition. Stir in the sour cream and vanilla. In another bowl, sift together the baking powder, baking soda, salt (if using), and flour. Stir dry ingredients into the batter until well blended.

In another bowl, combine the streusel ingredients.

Pour half the batter into the prepared pan and sprinkle with half the streusel. Pour the remaining batter into the pan and top with the rest of the streusel. Bake for 50 minutes to 1 hour, or until a toothpick comes out clean when inserted in the center.

Sugar Cookies

Here is a delicious alternative to store-bought cookies—if you have the time to make your own.

MAKES 3 DOZEN

8 tablespoons (1 stick) salted butter, melted
1 cup sugar
1 whole egg
2 egg yolks
1 to 1½ cups all-purpose flour
½ teaspoon baking soda
Pinch of salt
Additional sugar to sprinkle on cookies

Combine the butter and sugar and beat until creamy. Add the egg and egg yolks and beat well. In a separate bowl, mix together the flour, baking soda, and salt. Gradually add to the butter mixture, using only enough of the flour mixture to make a dough you can roll. Beat well until the mixture holds together. Form into two balls; wrap them in aluminum foil or waxed paper and refigerate for several hours.

Preheat the oven to 400°F. Remove the dough from the refrigerator and roll out very thin on a floured board. Cut into shapes with cookie cutters, sprinkle with granulated sugar, and place on greased baking sheets.

Bake for 10 minutes, or until the cookies are just golden around the edges. Cool on wire rack or large plate.

FIRESIDE TEA FOR TWO

M E N U

FOR TWO

Mrs. Fleming's Irish Soda Bread

Wheatmeal Bread

Crumpets

Alice Morton's Seville Orange Marmalade

Crock of Sweet Butter

Assam Tea

FIRESIDE TEA FOR TWO

What better way to spend a cool fall evening at home with someone special? Crumpets toasted over the open fire, freshly baked Irish soda bread, crocks of tangy marmalade and sweet butter—it's no wonder that these simple, nourishing foods have become classics. A pot of savory Assam tea rounds out the pleasure.

MRS. FLEMING'S IRISH SODA BREAD

An easy, traditional favorite, good hot or toasted.

MAKES ONE 8-INCH ROUND LOAF

3½ cups all-purpose flour
½ cup sugar
1 teaspoon salt
½ teaspoon baking soda
2 teaspoons baking powder
2 large eggs, beaten
1 pint sour cream
1 cup dark raisins
2 teaspoons caraway seeds

Preheat the oven to 350°F. Grease and flour a round 8-inch cake pan.

Mix together the flour, sugar, salt, baking soda, and baking powder. Fold in the eggs and sour cream. Add the raisins and caraway seeds. Do not overbeat.

Pour the batter into the prepared pan. Smooth the surface and use a knife to cut a cross on the top of the dough. Bake for about 1 hour, or until the loaf sounds hollow when tapped on the bottom. Remove from pan and cool on a wire rack.

WHEATMEAL BREAD

Here's another loaf to try, instead of soda bread. Wheatmeal can be bought at any health food store.

MAKES ONE 8-INCH ROUND LOAF

3 cups all-purpose flour
1½ cups ground wheatmeal
1 teaspoon baking powder
8 tablespoons (1 stick) butter or
*   margarine, cut into small bits and*
*   softened*
Pinch of salt
Approximately 1¼ cups buttermilk

Preheat the oven to 350°F. Grease an 8-inch round cake pan. Mix the flour, wheatmeal, and baking powder in a large bowl, and cut in the butter until the mixture resembles meal. Stir in enough of the buttermilk until the mixture masses together to make a soft dough. On a well-floured kneading board, knead the dough for about 30 seconds and quickly shape into a firm ball.

Press the dough into the pan and cut a cross with a sharp knife from side to side of the pan. Bake for approximately 45 minutes or until a crust has formed and it sounds hollow when tapped on the bottom.

CRUMPETS

Crumpets are a seasonal delicacy in England, sold only during the cold months from September to April.

MAKES 6

1 teaspoon active dry yeast
1 teaspoon sugar
¼ cup warm water
⅓ cup milk
1 egg, lightly beaten
4 tablespoons (½ stick) butter, melted
1 cup all-purpose unsifted flour
½ teaspoon salt

Mix the yeast with the sugar; then add the water and let stand for about 5 minutes until foamy. Stir in the milk, egg, and 1 tablespoon of the butter. Add the flour and salt. Mix until well blended, cover with a damp towel, and let stand in a warm place until almost doubled (about 45 minutes).

Brush the insides of four 3-inch flan rings (or tunafish cans with both ends removed) and the bottom of a heavy frying pan or griddle with melted butter. Over low heat, heat the rings in the pan and then place about 2 tablespoons of batter into each. Cook for 7 minutes, or until holes appear and the tops are dry. Then remove the rings and turn the crumpets to brown them lightly on the other side (about 2 minutes). Repeat the process with the remaining batter. Crumpets are best served warm, but can also be cooled on a wire rack and toasted just before serving.

ALICE MORTON'S SEVILLE ORANGE MARMALADE

If you can't find bitter oranges, just substitute navel or temple oranges.

MAKES TWELVE 8-OUNCE JARS

12 medium-size bitter oranges
4 lemons
3 quarts of water
  Approximately 8 cups sugar (see below for amount)

Slice the oranges and lemons paper-thin. Remove the seeds and tie them in a square of cheesecloth. Put the orange and lemon slices in a large enamel or stainless steel bowl. Add the bag with the seeds to the bowl. Fill with water and macerate for 24 hours.

After it has macerated, put the fruit and seeds mixture into a large saucepan. Bring to a boil, reduce the heat to low, and simmer gently until the peel is soft (1 hour or more). Then discard the bag of seeds. Measure the liquid, and add 1 cup of sugar for every cup of fruit. Return to the saucepan and stir constantly over the heat until mixture comes to a second boil. Then let stand for another 24 hours in a bowl.

On the third day, put the marmalade in a saucepan and bring to a boil. Then lower the heat and simmer gently until the oranges are translucent (about 2 hours). Test for jelly consistency by letting drops form on the edge of a spoon; or place a little on a saucer and put briefly in the refrigerator to see if it will wrinkle when touched.

When ready, skim off the foam, pour into twelve 8-ounce sterilized jars, and fill and seal (see instructions page 9).

A selection of tea leaves *(clockwise from top left)*: Ceylon Orange Pekoe, Jasmine with flowers, Gunpowder, Ceylon Broken Orange Pekoe, Assam Golden Flowery Orange Pekoe, and Peach Blossom Oolong.

TEA TASTING

    Teas are like fine wines in that their qualities reflect where they are grown; altitude, climate, soil, all affect the taste of a leaf. Different growing regions yield distinctive varieties of tea, while the processes by which the leaves are prepared result in the three designations—black, oolong, and green teas. Black teas, the most popular in America, have been crushed, then fermented, before being dried. Oolong teas are only partially fermented; then they are steamed so the leaf

is a lighter green-brown. And green teas are merely steamed, preserving their leafy color.

Most teas we are familiar with have been blended to achieve a uniform taste and quality, as shipments of teas vary with the season and the source. Twenty-five or thirty different tea leaves may go into a supermarket favorite, while even a master tea labeled Darjeeling may, in fact, be made from a combination of leaves to achieve a Darjeeling-like taste at an affordable price. Blends are often a closely guarded company secret, and the tea tasters hold the key to their success.

Master tea tasters have built up an ability to identify between 1,500 and 1,600 teas, summing up their source, how they were prepared, at what season they were picked. (One expert at Twinings could even name the elevation at which the leaves were grown.) Hand and eye are employed before a sip is taken; moisture content and color in the unbrewed tea are important. Boiling water is added, and the sample steeped in a small pot for about 5 minutes before the liquid is poured into a white porcelain bowl where the color can be studied, with the leaves in a nearby strainer for further observation. Only then does the taster loudly slurp some to shower his palate with liquid, allowing him to judge quality, character, and age of the tea, before spitting out his mouthful. Tasters have developed a colorful vocabulary for their craft: The moment when boiling water is added to the tea is the "agony of the leaves." They characterize a leaf as "biscuity," for instance—with a yeasty aroma— or "round"—lacking in harshness, with excellent strength and color. But some of the major types of tea are known to us in this way:

Assam: These wild tea plants were found growing in the 1830s in the northeastern Indian province of Assam by Scotsman Robert Bruce. Until then, all tea

came to the west from China. The teas are dark, hearty, and pungent.

Ceylon: Any tea from Sri Lanka, with some variance in quality. Sir Thomas Lipton built his fortune on plantations there. The best teas are grown at high elevations and are full of fragrance and flavor.

Darjeeling: One of the finest teas in the world, it grows high in the mountains near Nepal—and its price is equally high. Professionals describe the flavor as that of black currants or muscat grapes.

Earl Grey: A blend of black teas with a distinctive taste from oil of bergamot, an Italian citrus fruit.

English Breakfast: A blend of strong teas from India and Ceylon, for a good start to the morning.

Formosa Oolong: Sparkling and irresistible, with a slightly peachy flavor. Grown on small family farms in Taiwan.

Gunpowder: Chinese green tea in which each leaf has been tightly rolled after being picked; the tighter the roll, the more expensive the tea. Delicate and subtle in flavor and fragrance.

Jasmine: Green or a mix of black and green tea, with jasmine flowers added.

Lady Londonderry: A black, blended tea made for a society hostess in the days when individuals ordered unique blends.

Lapsang Souchong: Originally from China, "Souchong" refers to its large leaf size. This tea is hearty, smoky, and rich in flavor.

Orange Pekoe: A popular term that means very little. "Pekoe" is simply a grade of leaf size—small—and the China original was, perhaps, flavored with orange blossom. Now a black tea that varies wildly in flavor depending on origin and processing.

THE ENGLISH HOTEL TEA

Tea at the Savoy Hotel in London.

MENU

FOR TWO

Assorted Tea Sandwiches

Scones with Devon Clotted Cream
and Strawberry Preserves
(SEE PAGE 9)

Blueberry and Peach Tart

Meringues with Strawberries and Cream

Chocolate Éclairs

China or Indian Tea

A tea dance at London's Waldorf Hotel.

THE ENGLISH HOTEL TEA

It's five o'clock at London's Waldorf Hotel and the Palm Court is aglow, full of fox-trotting couples who've come to enjoy a tea dance. And over at the Savoy, a man and a woman draw near at a table covered with blush pink napery and plates of warm scones top-heavy with cream. Waiters pour from gleaming pots—"China or Indian?"—then return with tiered stands of watercress sandwiches and tiny tarts. Teatime in one of London's top hotels, a tradition that dates to the early years of this century, is a ritual full of romance and ceremony, with full attention paid to each luxurious detail, from the teaware to the sandwiches and pastry.

BLUEBERRY AND PEACH TART

(From the Savoy Restaurant kitchen)

MAKES APPROXIMATELY
2 DOZEN

SWEET PASTRY

½ pound (2 sticks) unsalted butter,
   softened
½ cup sugar
   Pinch of salt
1 egg yolk
1½ cups all-purpose flour

PASTRY CREAM

2 cups milk
1 whole egg
3 egg yolks
½ cup sugar
6 tablespoons all-purpose flour
½ teaspoon vanilla extract or to taste
   Scant ½ cup thinly sliced peaches
½ cup blueberries
2 tablespoons apricot purée or strained
   preserves

To make the sweet pastry, cream the butter, sugar, and salt together. Add egg yolk; then add flour. Mix until smooth. Form the dough into a ball, cover with wax paper, and chill in the refrigerator for at least 1 hour.

Roll out pastry ¼ inch thick. Using a sharp knife, cut out 3- to 4-inch rounds and press them into 2- or 3-inch greased tart pans.

Preheat the oven to 350°F.

Place the pans in the refrigerator and chill for at least 30 minutes. Bake the tart shells empty for 10 minutes or until golden brown. Allow to cool.

To make pastry cream, put milk in saucepan and let come to the boil, and then cool slightly. Cream the egg, egg yolks, and sugar together. Add the flour, vanilla, and a little of the hot milk to blend. Add the egg-sugar mixture to the pan and cook, stirring, until it is thick and smooth like a custard. Cover with a sheet of wax paper and let the mixture cool.

When cool, fill the tarts halfway with pastry cream and top with two thin slices of peach and some fresh blueberries.

Bring some apricot purée to the boil. (If purée is not available, preserves mixed with water to give them a spreading consistency may be used, but they must be strained.) Allow to cool and brush over the fruit.

MERINGUES WITH STRAWBERRIES AND CREAM

(From the Savoy Restaurant kitchen)

Choose whatever berry is at its peak, but the contrast of strawberries and snowy meringue is delectable.

MAKES APPROXIMATELY 18

1 cup egg whites (approximately 6 eggs)
2 cups superfine sugar
2 cups heavy cream, whipped
1 pint fresh strawberries, halved

For an electric stove or a gas stove without a pilot light, preheat the oven to 200°F.

Whisk the egg whites until soft peaks form. Add the sugar and beat until stiff. Pipe 3- to 4-inch circles of meringue onto a baking sheet topped with a sheet of buttered parchment paper. If you have a gas stove with a pilot light, dry in the oven overnight by using the heat from the light; if you have an electric stove or a gas stove without a pilot light, bake the meringues for approximately 90 minutes, taking care that they do not begin to color, until dried out.

When cool and dry, pipe whipped cream on top of each meringue and garnish with fresh strawberry halves. If making the meringues ahead of time, store them in an airtight container.

CHOCOLATE ÉCLAIRS

(from the Savoy Restaurant kitchen)

MAKES APPROXIMATELY 16

CHOUX PASTRY

1 cup milk
8 tablespoons (1 stick) butter
¼ cup sugar
½ teaspoon vanilla extract
2 cups all-purpose flour
   Pinch of salt
5 eggs

WHIPPED CREAM FILLING

2 cups heavy cream
3 teaspoons vanilla extract
6–8 ounces semisweet chocolate

Preheat the oven to 350°F.

In a large saucepan, cook the milk, butter, sugar, and vanilla until the butter melts. Add flour and salt, and stir over low heat; the mixture will pull away from the sides of the pan and form a ball. Continue cooking, stirring constantly, until there is a film on the bottom of the pan. Place the mixture in the bowl of an electric mixer and allow to cool slightly. When cool, add the eggs one at a time, beating well after each addition.

Place in a pastry bag and pipe 3- to 4-inch long éclair shapes onto a greased baking sheet. Bake for 30 minutes. Remove from the oven and, when cold, split open horizontally with a sharp knife. Whip the heavy cream with vanilla. Melt the chocolate in top of a double boiler. Fill the éclairs with piped whipped cream and coat with melted chocolate.

MENU

FOR FOUR

Ginger Bears

Spiced Blueberry Jam

Annemarie's Carrot Cupcakes

Jelly Sandwiches

Cinnamon Toast

Cambric Tea

A PROPER CHILDREN'S TEA

Nursery tea in a traditional British home was the time for solid fare like boiled eggs, brown bread and butter, and a slice of cake, to be eaten under Nanny's observant eye. But any child would also enjoy these special treats, like whimsical ginger bear cookies and carrot cupcakes with creamy icing. Slice the sandwiches into heart shapes and cut the toast with cookie cutters, for added appeal. And a small celebrant would feel very grownup indeed if offered cambric tea—a light brew of tea to which lots and lots of milk, and a bit of sugar, is added.

GINGER BEARS

These chewy, spicy cookies are all-time nursery favorites.

MAKES 2 DOZEN

¾ cup shortening
1 cup dark brown sugar
¼ cup molasses
1 egg
2¼ cups all-purpose flour
2 teaspoons baking soda
½ teaspoon salt
1 teaspoon ground ginger
1 teaspoon ground cinnamon
1 teaspoon ground cloves
Granulated sugar

Preheat oven to 350°F.

Cream together the shortening, brown sugar, molasses, and egg. Sift the rest of the ingredients together (except the granulated sugar) and stir them into the molasses mixture.

Form the dough into 3 sizes of balls, to create body (large ball), head (medium ball), and ears, arms, and legs (small balls). Roll the balls in granulated sugar. Put figures together on greased baking sheets, allowing 2 inches between them. Bake approximately 12 mintues, until springy to the touch.

SPICED BLUEBERRY JAM

The spices make this jam uniquely flavorful and aromatic.

MAKES ABOUT TEN 8-OUNCE JARS

4–6 pints fresh blueberries
2 tablespoons fresh lemon juice
7 cups sugar
1 tablespoon ground cinnamon
1 teaspoon ground cloves
1 teaspoon ground allspice
1 packet (3 ounces) Certo

Wash, dry, and pick over the berries. Crush enough berries by hand or by quickly pulsing in a food processor to produce 6 cups.

In a large nonaluminum pot, combine the ingredients except the Certo, taking care to fill the pot only one-third full.

Bring to a full boil and cook over high heat, stirring constantly with a stainless-steel spoon, for 1 minute. Remove from the heat.

Stir in the Certo. Skim off the foam with a metal spoon and discard it.

Prepare ten 8-ounce glass canning jars and fill and seal (see instructions page 9).

ANNEMARIE'S CARROT CUPCAKES

Fresh peaches as well as carrots give these cupcakes their sweet taste.

MAKES 2 DOZEN

1½ *cups sugar*
1½ *cups vegetable oil*
  4 *eggs*
  1 *cup whole wheat flour*
  1 *cup all-purpose flour*
  2 *teaspoons baking soda*
  1 *teaspoon salt*
  2 *teaspoons ground cinnamon*
  1 *cup grated carrots*
  1 *cup sliced fresh peaches*
½ *cup chopped walnuts*

FROSTING

  8 *ounces cream cheese, softened*
2⅔ *cups confectioners' sugar*
¼ *pound (1 stick) unsalted butter, at room temperature*
  Candied violets (optional), for decoration

Preheat oven to 325°F.

To make the cupcakes, mix the sugar, oil, and eggs together. Sift the dry ingredients together and add to the egg mixture. Mix in the carrots, peaches, and nuts. Place in well-greased muffin or cupcake pans, and bake for 30 to 40 minutes, or until springy to the touch. Frost and decorate with candied violets, if desired.

To make the frosting, cream together the cream cheese, confectioners' sugar, and butter until smooth.

When the cupcakes are cool, frost them generously with the cream cheese mixture.

JELLY SANDWICHES

To please a child, cut the sandwiches in fanciful shapes with cookie cutters or slice them in long narrow strips, triangles, squares, and circles.

Sliced white bread
Butter
Strawberry jelly, or blueberry jam

Trim the crusts off the bread, then spread one slice very lightly with butter, and top with strawberry jelly and the other slice of bread.

CINNAMON TOAST

A loaf of fresh bread, sliced then toasted, is a good platform for a variety of child-pleasers.

Sliced white bread
Butter
Sugar
Cinnamon

Toast a slice of bread, then butter one side. Mix together 1 tablespoon sugar with ½ teaspoon cinnamon, and sprinkle on the bread. Then broil just until the sugar caramelizes on the bread.

MENU

FOR FIVE

Mrs. Foley's Shortbread Squares

Dundee Cake

Rich Dark Fruitcake

Frosted Grapes

Marzipan Fruits

Sherry and Walnuts

Lady Londonderry Tea

WINTER HOLIDAY TEA

A very proper parlor, this, where friends might gather after a mad dash of shopping or an afternoon concert. Or meet on New Year's Day for a formal, gracious tea that's full of the spirit of celebration. Guests would share rich cakes and lavish tarts, and frosted grapes and glowing candied fruits. One's best is surely called for—crisp white linens, a shining silver salver, a tea set in fine French porcelain, perhaps, with a teapot full of Lady Londonderry tea.

MRS. FOLEY'S SHORTBREAD SQUARES

Scotland's favorite, this cookie requires the very best fresh butter for its flavor.

MAKES 2 DOZEN

1 cup confectioners' sugar
1 pound (4 sticks) salted butter, softened
4½ cups all-purpose flour

Preheat the oven to 325°F.

Blend the confectioners' sugar into the butter, and then gradually add the flour, 1 cup at a time. Dough will be very thick. Place dough on floured surface, pat down, and roll out ¼ to ½ inch thick. Cut into 2½-inch squares, and place on an ungreased baking sheet. Prick the top of each square with a fork. Bake at 325°F. for 25 to 30 minutes; cookies should be pale on top, but golden brown on the bottom. Remove from oven and cool on wire racks. Store in an airtight container.

DUNDEE CAKE

The Scots are great bakers, and Dundee is famous for its cake full of preserved fruit and nuts.

MAKES ONE 9-INCH ROUND OR
8-INCH SQUARE CAKE

½ pound (2 sticks) salted butter, softened
1 cup sugar
Grated rind of 2 oranges
5 eggs, beaten
2½ cups all-purpose flour
1 teaspoon baking powder
Pinch of salt
¼ cup blanched almonds, chopped
1 cup dark raisins
1 cup dried currants
½ cup chopped mixed candied citrus peel
1½ tablespoons strained orange juice
Extra blanched almonds for decoration

Preheat the oven to 300°F. Grease a 9-inch round deep cake pan or an 8-inch square pan; line the bottom with brown paper and grease the paper; then line with wax paper.

Cream the butter with the sugar and orange rind. Gradually beat in the eggs until light and fluffy.

Sift together the flour, baking powder, and salt. Mix in the chopped almonds, raisins, currants, and candied peel. Stir into the creamed mixture with the orange juice. Pour the batter into the prepared pan. Smooth the surface and arrange the extra almonds in a pattern on top.

Bake for 2 hours, or until a toothpick inserted in the center of the cake comes out clean. Cool in the pan.

RICH DARK FRUITCAKE

Kept in an airtight container and dabbed with brandy, this cake can be sliced and served for two weeks or more.

MAKES TWO 10-INCH ROUND CAKES

1½ pounds dried currants
1½ pounds golden raisins
1½ pounds dark raisins
½ cup plus 5 tablespoons brandy
1 pound (4 sticks) salted butter
2 cups dark brown sugar
8 large eggs
1 cup mixed candied citrus peel
½ cup slivered almonds
2 cups all-purpose flour
½ cup rice flour
2 teaspoons baking soda
1 teaspoon salt
2 teaspoons ground cinnamon
1 teaspoon each of ground ginger, ground cloves, ground allspice, and ground mace
Additional brandy to sprinkle on top of cake

Sprinkle the fruit with the ½ cup brandy, cover with plastic wrap, and let stand for a least 2 hours.

Preheat the oven to 300°F. Grease 2 10-inch-deep round cake pans; line the bottoms first with greased brown paper and then with greased wax paper.

Cream the butter and sugar with an electric mixer. Add the eggs one at a time, beating well after each addition. Add the brandy-soaked fruit, candied peel, and almonds. Mix together the dry ingredients and fold them in.

Pour the batter into the prepared pans. Bake for 4 to 5 hours, until a toothpick inserted in the center comes out clean. Remove from the oven and, while the cakes are still hot, sprinkle 2½ tablespoons of brandy on each. Allow to cool in the pans, well wrapped in wax paper and a cotton dish towel and then in several thicknesses of newspaper. This lets the cakes cool very slowly so that the brandy doesn't evaporate and the many flavors have time to blend together. Remove from pan, wrap well in wax paper, and store in a cake tin in a cool, dry place. Sprinkle the cakes all over with brandy every few days and rewrap tightly. Serve in small portions, as the cake is very rich.

FROSTED GRAPES

Currants can replace grapes for an attractive and tasty variation.

2 egg whites
Large bunch of seedless grapes
Sugar

Whisk the egg whites very lightly, being careful not to let a lot of bubbles form. Using a brush, coat the grapes with the egg whites. Then place the grapes in a shallow dish and pour the sugar over them. Gently roll the grapes in the sugar to coat them completely.

CHRISTMAS EVE TEA

MENU

FOR FOUR

Loafer's Classic English Trifle

Cream Roses

Brandy Snaps

Champagne

Russian Caravan Tea

CHRISTMAS EVE TEA

The tea table is glittering with the sumptuous delights of the Christmas season. Crystal and silver baskets are mounded with delicious sweets, many based on England's most traditional recipes. The lavish treats are matched by their setting, a table placed in a corner, with its French linen wallcoverings and rich Oriental rug. There's gleaming majolica, a traditional silver service, napkins edged with ecru lace, and mercury glass vases and candlesticks that lend sparkle. Surely these riches are appropriate to an aromatic and full-bodied tea like Russian Caravan.

LOAFER'S CLASSIC ENGLISH TRIFLE
(By pastry chef Donna Potter-Astin)

Trifles have been popular in England since the eighteenth century and deserve the very prettiest bowls.

SERVES 10

¼ cup sugar
2 tablespoons cornstarch
4 egg yolks
1 cup milk
2 cups heavy cream
1 teaspoon vanilla
2 packages ladyfingers
1 cup raspberry preserves combined with
   ¼ cup framboise
½ cup sweet or medium dry sherry

WHIPPED CREAM GARNISH (OPTIONAL)

1 cup heavy cream
2 teaspoons vanilla extract

In the top of a double boiler over gently simmering water, mix the sugar, cornstarch, and egg yolks. Heat, stirring, until warm. In a separate saucepan, heat milk and 1 cup of the heavy cream until warm; add to the mixture in the double boiler. Stir constantly, until the mixture has thickened significantly and coats the back of a spoon. Never let the mixture come to a boil, and be sure that the water in the bottom of the double boiler remains barely simmering at all times.

Remove from the heat and stir in the vanilla. Allow the mixture to cool, stirring occasionally to release steam and excess heat. Whip the remaining cup of heavy cream and fold it into the cooled custard until smooth.

To assemble the trifle, spread the split ladyfingers with raspberry preserves that have been softened with framboise. Sandwich the ladyfingers together and cut crosswise into halves. Line the bottom and sides of a glass or crystal bowl decoratively with half of the ladyfingers. Sprinkle with ¼ cup of the sherry (use sweet or medium dry, depending on taste). Pour in half the custard, cover with plastic wrap, and allow it to chill in the refrigerator until partially set. Then repeat the procedure by layering the remaining ladyfingers, sherry, and custard on top. Cover and chill until set, preferably overnight.

Make the whipped cream garnish just prior to serving. Whip the heavy cream and vanilla together until stiff. Pipe decoratively on top of the trifle with a rosette tip.

CREAM ROSES

Practice forming the roses on a bit of wax paper first.

MAKES 2 CUPS OR ENOUGH
TO FILL 16 TARTLET SHELLS

3 cups fresh strawberries, washed, dried, and hulled
1 teaspoon (1/2 package) unflavored gelatin
1 cup heavy cream
Approximately 3 tablespoons confectioners' sugar
16 Tartlet Shells (page 16)

Purée the strawberries in a food processor. Sprinkle the gelatin on top, and pour the purée into a saucepan. Stir gently over very low heat until the gelatin dissolves. Let the purée cool to lukewarm.

Combine the cream with 3 tablespoons confectioners' sugar (use slightly more if berries are tart) and whip until the cream is very thick. Fold in the lukewarm strawberry purée. Pipe the mixture in the shape of a rose into the tartlet shells. Put the tartlets in the refrigerator for at least 2 hours, until set. Store cream roses in the refrigerator; serve chilled.

BRANDY SNAPS

These crisp sweets have the delectably rich flavor of carmelized sugar.

MAKES ABOUT 3 DOZEN 2-INCH COOKIES

8 tablespoons (1 stick) salted butter
1/2 cup sugar
1/3 cup dark molasses
1/4 teaspoon ground ginger
1/2 teaspoon ground cinnamon
1/2 teaspoon grated lemon rind
1 cup all-purpose flour
2 teaspoons brandy

Preheat the oven to 325°F.

In a saucepan over very low heat, combine the butter, sugar, molasses, ginger, cinnamon, and lemon rind until blended. Remove from the heat and add the flour and brandy. Gather into a ball and wrap in wax paper. Chill the dough in the refrigerator for 20 to 30 minutes.

Roll rounded teaspoonfuls of dough into balls, and place 2 inches apart on an ungreased baking sheet. Bake on the bottom rack of the oven for about 12 minutes, until cookies are lacy thin and lightly browned.

Maids of Honour

THE TEA-ROOM TRADITION

An English tea room is as much a neighborhood institution as the red postbox on the corner; whether a friendly local spot serving up home-baked goodies by a coal fire, or one of the grand tea palaces with potted palms and string orchestra sawing away, for years they were the source of something more than simply sustenance. Shoppers in town for the day stopped by to rest their bundles—and their feet. Children came and lapped the whipped cream from their

fairy cakes as a treat after the dentist. Women shuffled off their home chores for the moment and met their best friends for a companionable cup and a chat.

What became the middle-class woman's bastion can be traced back, it's said, to the eighteenth century when a woman named Maria Twek opened an unlicensed tea shop—women were forbidden tea licenses—and refused to shut it, though fined time and again. Tea gardens became popular in London in the mid-eighteenth century and remained in vogue until the last one closed a hundred years later and places for the public enjoyment of tea disappeared. Certainly both the upper classes and working people continued to brew their pots at home, but no longer could this nation of tea drinkers easily enjoy a cup outside the home.

By the 1880s, the tea shops' time had come. In London, an enterprising manager of a bake shop belonging to the Associated Bread Company invited friends and a few customers to share some tea in the back of the store—then urged ABC to spread the practice. Within just a few years there were ABC tea shops everywhere, as well as other chains, providing a good, cheap tea with all the accoutrements. Women's increasing mobility in the big cities underwrote the shops' success—the young working women or matrons out for the day welcomed a place where they could eat alone, inexpensively and discreetly.

Perhaps the most famous of the tea shop chains was that of Lyons, 250 shops full of democratic glamour—the orchestra, the palms—that held a firm place in the English heart. Their waitresses, called "nippies," nipped around cheerily with their overladen trays of steaming pots and tea sandwiches and cakes.

There are still places that capture the glamour, the joy of times past. Fortnum and Mason's tea room hums throughout the day, and lots of people go to the Maids of Honour tea room, in the Richmond area of London, to enjoy the chintz and Windsor chairs, as well as the old family recipe for Henry VIII's favorite cakes. And the Willow Tea Room in Glasgow, with its extraordinary designs by Charles Rennie Mackintosh, draws the shopper and explorer alike. The tea shop will serve its cup of cheer for all time.

MENU

FOR THREE

Mrs. Pettigrew's Lemon Cake

Coffee and Walnut Cake

Park Pies

Ceylon Tea

THIRTIES-STYLE TEA ROOM

Tea-Time, in the cozy neighborhood of Clapham in London, is a tidy, tiny evocation of the glory days of the tea shop. To the music of Cole Porter playing softly in the background, waitresses clad in fetching thirties-style uniforms buzz about with cakes and sandwiches served up on china that has the clean, spare lines and flowery decoration of the era. Customers love to lounge in the period Lloyd loom chairs and dawdle over homey, comfortable treats like the tea shop's good lemon cake, coffee and walnut cake, and Park pies.

MRS. PETTIGREW'S LEMON CAKE

This solid cake is a treasure from an English tea room.

MAKES ONE 7-INCH ROUND CAKE OR 8-INCH LOAF

2 lemons
¾ cup sugar
8 tablespoons (1 stick) salted butter or margarine, softened
2 large eggs, beaten
¾ cup all-purpose flour
6 tablespoons milk
3 tablespoons sugar, for topping

Preheat the oven to 325°F. Grease and line a 7-inch round cake pan or 8-inch loaf pan with parchment or wax paper.

Grate the lemon rinds and set aside. Combine the juice of 1 lemon with 3 tablespoons sugar in a bowl and set in a warm place until the sugar dissolves and forms a syrup with the juice.

Cream the margarine and the rest of the sugar together until light and fluffy. Add the beaten eggs, a little at a time, beating well after each addition. Stir in the grated lemon rind and flour; beat again thoroughly (the longer you beat, the softer the cake). Add the milk and beat again.

Pour into the prepared pan and bake for at least 1 hour; the cake should spring back when pressed gently in the center. Immediately upon removing the cake from the oven, prick the top with a long-tined fork or thin skewer and pour the lemon juice–sugar syrup all over the top until completely covered. Cool in the pan to allow the syrup to be soaked up and create a moist and tangy cake.

COFFEE AND WALNUT CAKE

A rich, sweet layer cake, iced and filled with coffee frosting, is accented with nuts.

MAKES ONE 7-INCH LAYER CAKE

½ cup plus 2 tablespoons all-purpose flour
1 teaspoon baking powder
½ teaspoon salt
½ cup plus 2 tablespoons granulated sugar
10 tablespoons (1¼ sticks) unsalted butter, softened
3 large eggs
2½ tablespoons powdered instant espresso coffee or 1 teaspoon coffee extract
¼ cup plus 2 tablespoons walnuts, chopped

FILLING AND FROSTING

1 cup confectioners' sugar
12 tablespoons (1½ sticks) unsalted butter, softened
1 tablespoon Kahlua or strong coffee
9 or 10 walnut halves, for decoration

Preheat the oven to 350°F. Grease and line two 7-inch round cake pans with parchment or wax paper.

Sift together the flour, baking powder, and salt. In a separate bowl, beat the sugar and butter until light and fluffy. Add the eggs one at a time, adding 1 tablespoon of the flour mixture after each. Beat well after each addition.

Mix in the remaining flour and beat thoroughly. Then stir in the coffee and walnuts. Turn into the prepared cake pans and bake for 35 to 40 minutes, until lightly browned.

Remove from the oven and leave in the pans for a few minutes. Then turn out onto a wire rack to cool completely.

To make the filling, beat together the confectioners' sugar, butter, and Kahlua until very smooth. Then sandwich the two layers together with the filling, frost, and decorate with the walnut halves.

PARK PIES

The name of these little pies reflects the tea room's location across from the greenery of Clapham Common.

MAKES 16

FILLING

1 cup chopped pitted dates
2 tablespoons water
2 tablespoons dark brown sugar
Juice of 1 lemon
Grated rind of 2 lemons

PASTRY CRUST

1 cup all-purpose flour
1 teaspoon baking soda
1 cup rolled oats
¾ cup plus 2 tablespoons dark brown sugar
12 tablespoons (1½ sticks) salted butter, melted
Juice of 1 lemon

Preheat the oven to 375°F. Grease 16 regular size muffin pans.

To make the filling, put into a small saucepan the dates, water, sugar, lemon juice, and rind. Bring to a boil and simmer gently, uncovered, until thick and smooth but not dry. Stir occasionally. Remove from the heat and cool.

To make the pastry crust, mix together the flour, baking soda, oats, and sugar. Add the melted butter and lemon juice. Blend together using a fork or floured hands. Roll the dough out about ¼ inch thick on a floured board, and divide it into three portions. Cut two thirds of the dough into sixteen 3-inch circles and pat them into the base and sides of the pans; cut the remaining dough into sixteen 1½-inch circles.

Put 1 to 2 teaspoonfuls of the date mixture into the pastry shells and set the 1½-inch circles of dough on top, pressing the edges together. Bake for 35 minutes, or until lightly browned. Remove from the oven, cool in the tins, and then lift out onto a wire rack.

THE TEA LARDER

TEA TRIMMINGS

A bit of milk, some sugar—one lump or two?—those are the traditional partners for a cup of tea. But it's fun to experiment with a few variations on them.

Crystallized ginger—sugar's sweetness, with an added flavor

Honey—clover's fine, but try elderflower, wild flower, cream honey

Lemon—slice it paper thin, or stud the rind with circles of cloves

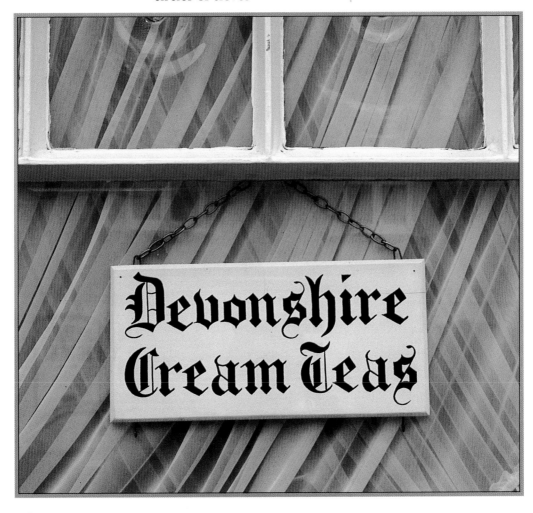

Mint—pick peppermint leaves or crush spearmint leaves and brew with the tea

Preserves—stir a bit of strawberry or cherry preserves into the cup the way the Russians and Hungarians do

Sugar—fill the bowl with cubes; brown sugars like madeira, French raw sugar cubes; pastel crystals; sugar that's been flavored with a vanilla bean (insert one bean into two cups of sugar, seal tightly, and allow to sit for a week before using)

FILLINGS, BREADS, AND SPREADS

Beyond the pleasures of traditional cress and cucumber, tea sandwiches may be filled with almost any filling that isn't so wet that it will soak through the bread. Consider using cream puffs, biscuits, scones, puff pastry shells, tartlets, muffins, and crêpes along with the traditional sandwich breads.

The simplest chicken, ham, or cheese sandwich will be enlivened by one of these tasty spreads.

Mayonnaise variations To a cup of mayonnaise, homemade or store-bought, add: 2 teaspoons Dijon mustard, or 1 tablespoon freshly chopped chives, or 2 teaspoons grated lemon rind or orange peel.

Butters To a stick of softened butter, fold in until the mixture reaches a creamy consistency: 4 ripe, hulled, and mashed strawberries, or 1 tablespoon freshly chopped tarragon or mixed herbs, or 2 tablespoons honey with grated rind of one lemon.

Cream cheeses To an 8-ounce package of cream cheese, softened, mix in: ¼ cup chopped dates, or ¼ cup chopped walnuts, hazelnuts, pecans, almonds, or raisins, or 2 tablespoons chives, chopped, or ¼ cup raspberry preserves, or 2 tablespoons diced scallions.

TEA SANDWICHES

Make up a quantity of sandwiches, and if you are not serving them right away, store them in the refrigerator for a few hours, either sealed in airtight plastic bags, or with a slightly damp dish towel draped over them.

Here are some interesting tea sandwiches to try in addition to those on page 11.

Smoked turkey with raspberry mayonnaise on cracked wheat bread

Curried chicken with walnuts on white bread

Shrimp with dill vinaigrette on oatmeal bread

Tomato with basil on black bread with home-made mayonnaise

Avocado with sprouts and walnuts on whole wheat bread

Sliced hard boiled eggs with cracked black pepper and bibb lettuce on wheat bread with herb mayonnaise

Stilton cheese crumbled over pear slices on oatmeal bread

Sugar-cured ham with thin pineapple slices on dill bread

Asparagus spears with lemon mayonnaise on wheat bread

Cream cheese with walnuts on date nut raisin bread

MAIL-ORDER TEA SOURCES

ANZEN PACIFIC CORPORATION
P.O. Box 11407
Portland, OR 97211
(503) 283-1284

BEWLEY'S IRISH IMPORTS
606 Howard Road
West Chester, PA 19380

BON APPETIT
212 South 17th Street
Philadelphia, PA 19103
(215) 546-8059

CAPITAL TEAS LIMITED
Tea Tasters Notebook and Catalog
of Superb Connoisseur Teas
61 Dolan Drive
Guilford, CT 06437

CHEESE COFFEE CENTER
2115 Allston Way
Berkeley, CA 94704
(415) 848-7115

CONTE DI SAVOIA
555 W. Roosevelt Road
Jeffro Plaza, Store # 7
Chicago, IL 60607
(312) 666-3471

THE DAILY GRIND
P.O. Box 607C
Nashville, IN 47448
(812) 988-4808

EGERTONS
Lyme Street
Axminster
Devon
England EX13 5DB

FORTNUM & MASON LTD.
Piccadilly
London
England W1A 1ER

GRACE TEA CO., LTD.
50 West 17th Street
New York, NY 10011
(212) 255-2935

J. BRADBURY & COMPANY, INC.
P.O. Box 2366
Grand Central Station
New York, NY 10163

LEKVAR-BY-THE-BARREL
H. Roth & Son
1577 First Avenue
New York, NY 10028
(212) 734-1110

NICHOLS GARDEN NURSERY
1190 North Pacific Highway
Albany, OR 97321
(503) 928-9280

O.H. CLAPP AND CO.
47 Riverside Drive
Westport, CT 06880
(203) 226-3301

OLD NORTH CHURCH
GIFT SHOP
193 Salem Street
Boston, MA 02113
(617) 523-6676

O'MONA INTERNATIONAL
TEA CO. LTD.
9 Pine Ridge Road
Rye Brook, NY 10573
(914) 937-8858

PAPRIKAS WEISS IMPORTER
1546 Second Avenue
New York, NY 10028
(212) 288-6903

THE PERFECT CUP
2525 Creighton
Garland, TX 75042

SCHAPIRA COFFEE COMPANY
117 West 10th Street
New York, NY 10011
(212) 675-3733

THE SENSUOUS BEAN
228 Columbus Avenue
New York, NY 10023
(212) 724-7725

SIMPSON AND VAIL
P.O. Box 309
Pleasantville, NY 10570
(914) 747-1336

SIMPSON AND VAIL, INC.
53 Park Place
New York, NY 10007

THE SIR THOMAS LIPTON
COLLECTION
Sir Thomas Lipton's
Trading Company
Mail Order Division
115 Brand Road
Salem, VA 24156
(703) 389-8336

SPECIALTY SPICE SHOP
2757 152nd Avenue, N.E. #4
Redmond, WA 98052

TEA TIMER—
A SOCIETY FOR TEA LOVERS
Suite 9
116 East 16th Street
New York, NY 10003

UWAJIMAYA
Sixth Avenue South and
South King Street
Seattle, WA 98104
(206) 624-6248

WALNUT ACRES
Penns Creek, PA 17862
(717) 837-0601

WHITTARD AND CO. LTD.
111 Fulham Road
London 6RP SW3
England

YOUNG & SAUNDERS LTD.
5 Queensferry Street
Edinburgh
Scotland EH2 4PD

Crumpets by Mail!

THE ENGLISH TEA SHOP
511 Irving Street
San Francisco, CA 94122
(415) 564-2255

Catering and at-home delivery . . .

TEA FOR TWO
Jennifer Lyons
181 East 73rd Street
New York, NY 10021
(212) 744-0001

Acknowledgments

I'd like to thank all those who made this book possible, especially Keith Scott Morton, who was always there for me and captured the essence of *Having Tea* so beautifully; Catherine Calvert, who told the story; Rita Marshall, who made our vision of it come to life and Etienne Delessert, whose drawings embellish it; Trish Penberthy, who provided us with her wonderful recipes; Mindy Drucker, who took care of all the details; Louise Natenshon, who tested everything for us; and Mardee Regan.

My appreciation also goes to Beth Friedman, Barbara Streicker, Sally Freedman, Annemarie Jason, Margaret Foley, Alice Morton, Elvira Fleming, Donna Potter-Astin, Margaret Ahern, and Mrs. Scotti, for sharing their recipes with us.

A special thank-you to my family who pitched in and helped whenever we needed it, especially Mom, Dad, Mary, and Mark; thanks, too, to K. C. Witherell, Bill Steele, Matthew Mattiello, and Fred Magro for their continued encouragement, as well as Lee Bailey and Mary Emmerling for their advice and enthusiasm.

I'd also like to express my gratitude to all the many people who opened their doors and shared their tea services with us: Bob McDaniel, Charles Braslow, Carolyn Guttilla, Sam Blount and Tom Fleming of Irvine and Fleming, Karen McCready, Glenna Craw, Hilda Gerstein, the Dominican Sisters of Villa Maria, and my friends in Yaphank: Lucille and Wally Stroud, Kathy Schmidt, Karen Moussakes, Ralph Silano, Carmela and Joe Hreachmack, Baer Lustgarden, and the Glovers.

To Nick Powell, who took care of us in London, as well as to all those at Twinings, the Savoy Hotel, the Waldorf Hotel, Mr. Newens of the Maids of Honour Tea Room, and especially to Jane Pettigrew and Clifford Lees of Tea-Time. To my agents, Deborah Geltman and Gayle Benderoff, who offered constant support.

And to all those at Clarkson N. Potter, especially Nancy Novogrod, Gael Towey, Jonathan Fox, Amy Boorstein, True Sims, Laurie Stark, Harvey-Jane Kowal, and Phyllis Fleiss, who kept us going! Thank you!

—Tricia Foley

INDEX

Alice Morton's Seville orange
    marmalade, 49
Annemarie's carrot cupcakes, 61
apple:
    butter, 41
    tarts, individual, 33
Assam tea, 47, 48, 52–53
Aunt Sally's Bundt cake, 45

black currant tea, 23, 24
black tea, 51
Bloody Marys, 41
blueberry:
    jam, spiced, 60
    and peach tarts, 56
Boston tea party, 4
brandy snaps, 69
breads, 80
    dark pumpernickel, 12
    Mrs. Fleming's Irish soda, 48
    oatmeal, 12–13
    wheatmeal, 48
Bruce, Robert, 52
brunch in the city, 38–41
Bundt cakes:
    Aunt Sally's, 45
    spicy ginger, 44
    sugar-glazed lemon, 24
    Victorian poppy seed, 13
buttermilk scones, 8
butters, 12, 47, 48, 80

cakes:
    Annemarie's carrot cupcakes, 61
    Aunt Sally's Bundt, 45
    coffee and walnut, 76–77
    Dundee, 64
    Mrs. Pettigrew's lemon, 76
    rich dark fruit, 65
    spicy ginger Bundt, 44
    sugar-glazed lemon, 24
    Victorian poppy seed, 13
cambric tea, 59, 60
carrot cupcakes, Annemarie's, 61
Ceylon tea, 53
cheese, leek and spinach flan, 32–33
chicken, honey-glazed, 28

children's tea, proper, 58–61
China tea, 53, 55, 56
Chinese, 2–3, 20
chocolate éclairs, 57
Christmas Eve tea, 66–69
cinnamon toast, 61
coffee and walnut cake, 76–77
cookies:
    brandy snaps, 69
    ginger bears, 60
    Mrs. Foley's shortbread squares,
      64
    sugar, 45
cornmeal muffins, 40
cream cheeses, 80
cream roses, 69
cream scones, 8
cream teas, 8
crumpets, 49
crystallized ginger, 79
cupcakes, Annemarie's carrot, 61

Darjeeling tea, 11, 12, 52, 53
dark pumpernickel bread, 12
de Quincy, Thomas, 44
dessert party tea, 14–17
Dundee cake, 64

Earl Grey tea, 43, 44, 53
éclairs, chocolate, 57
eggs, slow-scrambled, with cream
    and chives, 40
English, 3–4
English Breakfast tea, 39, 40, 53
English hotel tea, 54–57

fall tea in the country, 30–33
fireside tea for two, 46–49
flans, individual, 32–33
Formosa oolong tea, 53
Fortnum and Mason's tea room, 73
frosted grapes, 65
fruitcake, rich dark, 65

ginger:
    bears, 60
    Bundt cake, spicy, 44
    crystallized, 79
grandmother's strawberry jam, 9
grapes, frosted, 65
green tea, 37, 51, 52
Gunpowder tea, 53

ham and cheese flan, 32–33
Holland, 3
honey, 79
honey-glazed chicken, 28

iced tea, minted orange pekoe, 29
India tea, 52–53, 56
individual apple tarts, 33
individual flans, 32–33

jams:
    grandmother's strawberry, 9
    peach-orange, 25
    spiced blueberry, 60
Japan, 3
jasmine tea, 53
jelly sandwiches, 61
Johnson, Samuel, 4

Lady Londonderry tea, 53, 63, 64
Lapsang Soochong tea, 31, 32, 37,
    53
lemon:
    cake, Mrs. Pettigrew's, 76
    cake, sugar-glazed, 24
    curd tartlets, 16–17
lemons, 79
Lipton, Sir Thomas, 53
loaf, walnut tea, 25
loafer's classic English trifle, 68
Lyons tea shops, 73

Mackintosh, Charles Rennie, 73
Maids of Honour tea room, 73
marmalade, Alice Morton's Seville
    orange, 49
mayonnaise, variations on, 80

meringues with strawberries and cream, 57
mint, 80
minted iced orange pekoe tea, 29
Mrs. Fleming's Irish soda bread, 48
Mrs. Foley's shortbread squares, 64
Mrs. Pettigrew's lemon cake, 76
muffins, cornmeal, 40

oatmeal bread, 12–13
old-fashioned peach pie, 29
oolong tea, 51–52
orange:
    marmalade, Alice Morton's Seville, 49
    peach-, jam, 25
orange pekoe tea, 53
    minted iced, 27, 28, 29

pan-fried tomatoes with fresh tarragon, 41
Park pies, 76, 77
peach:
    -orange jam, 25
    pie, old-fashioned, 29
    tarts, blueberry and, 56
pies:
    old-fashioned peach, 29
    Park, 76, 77
poppy seed cake, Victorian, 13
potato salad, red, 28
preserves, fruit, 80
Prince of Wales tea, 15, 16
pumpernickel bread, dark, 12

Queen Mary tea, 7, 8

raisin scones, 9
raspberry:
    shortcake, 17
    sorbet with spearmint, 16
red potato salad, 28
rich dark fruit cake, 65
Russian Caravan tea, 67, 68

salad, red potato, 28
sandwiches, tea, 80–81
    assorted, 55, 56
    jelly, 61
    open-faced garden, 11, 12
    spreads and fillings for, 80
Savoy Hotel, 56, 57
scones:
    buttermilk, 8
    cream, 8
    raisin, 9
Shen Nung, 2–3
shortbread squares, Mrs. Foley's, 64
shortcake, raspberry, 17
slow-scrambled eggs with cream and chives, 40
sorbet, raspberry, with spearmint, 16
spiced blueberry jam, 60
spicy ginger Bundt cake, 44
spreads, 80
    apple butter, 41
    butters, 12, 47, 48, 80
    cream cheeses, 80
    mayonnaise variations, 80
strawberries and cream, meringues with, 57
strawberry cream tea, 6–9
strawberry jam, grandmother's, 9
sugar, 80
sugar cookies, 45
sugar-glazed lemon cake, 24
summer harvest picnic, 26–29
Sunday afternoon tea, 10–13

tartlets:
    cream roses, 69
    lemon curd, 16–17
tarts:
    blueberry and peach, 56
    individual apple, 33
tea:
    brewing of, 35–37
    larder for, 79–81
    pleasures of, 1–5
    services for, 19–21
    tasting of, 51–52
    tea rooms and, 71–77
tea break, 42–45
tea loaf, walnut, 25
tea on the lawn, 22–25

teapots, 2–3, 19–21
tearooms, 71–77
teas, types of, 51–53
    Assam, 47, 48, 52–53
    black, 51
    black currant, 23, 24
    cambric, 59, 60
    Ceylon, 53, 75
    China, 53, 55, 56
    Darjeeling, 11, 12, 52, 53
    Earl Grey, 43, 44, 53
    English Breakfast, 39, 40, 53
    Formosa oolong, 53
    green, 37, 51, 52
    Gunpowder, 53
    India, 52–53, 55, 56
    jasmine, 53
    Lady Londonderry, 53, 63, 64
    Lapsang Soochong, 31, 32, 37, 53
    oolong, 51–52
    orange pekoe, 27, 28, 29, 53
    Prince of Wales, 15, 16
    Queen Mary, 7, 8
    Russian Caravan, 67, 68
Tea-Time, 76
thirties-style tea rooms, 74–77
toast, cinnamon, 61
tomatoes:
    pan-fried, with fresh tarragon, 41
    vine-ripened, with fresh basil, 29
trifle, loafer's classic English, 68
Twek, Maria, 72
Twining, Sam, 4

Victorian poppy seed cake, 13

Waldorf Hotel, 56
walnut:
    cake, coffee and, 76–77
    tea loaf, 25
    wheatmeal bread, 48
Willow Tea Room, 73
winter holiday tea, 62–65

zucchini flan, 32–33

SOUTHAMPTON